Leave It Behind

by
Emily Raabe

~

*Finalist for the 2011 FutureCycle Poetry Book Prize
(Second Place)*

FUTURECYCLE PRESS
www.futurecycle.org

Leave It Behind

Published by FutureCycle Press
Mineral Bluff, Georgia, U.S.A.

ISBN: 978-0-9839985-0-1

For Norm Walker, teacher
And for always, Paul

4   LEAVE IT BEHIND

Contents

Beginning

We passed a lean-to somewhere in Scotland,
empty except for a pile of hay.
The hay bore a mark left deep by an animal.
This cow with its baby, two sheep in love, a vagrant
looking to sleep unmolested left behind them a sign of the body,
body in silence that shows itself
through emptiness
in the battened-down hay.

8   LEAVE IT BEHIND

I.

Here are your waters and your watering place.
Drink and be whole again beyond confusion.

—Robert Frost

10   LEAVE IT BEHIND

My Best Dream

goes like this: two fields
cut by a thin line of trees.

In the dream I'm at the line
when the storm comes in.

I dig a ditch in the dark
in the snow in the dream

and get in, and then
the animals arrive—

long noses, soft bodies,
raccoons maybe, deer,

bears, all the creatures
with night eyes

climb into my ditch
with deliberation, settle

their tails, snouts, paws,
speckled haunches

around and over me
so we are cuddled in

like kit fox kittens in a den.
There is no fear of freezing

in this dream, no muttered
counting off of time

because everything is here,
has arrived on padded feet

with something like love
in that it is the absence

of distance. We rest
warm in the sleep

we fear to allow ourselves,
not even on the darkest night,

not even with the snow
falling fast oh fast, and animals

so unafraid that they sleep
unfurled in your arms.

The dream, you understand me,
was a gift, but it came

with a price. I sleep each night
with my palms up

and wake
each morning alone.

Darwin in the Andes

All day today I've felt lucky: time is nice
instead of a yawning tunnel, the dog sighs
in her sleep at my feet, food is warm and eaten
off the good plates. I know I will pay

for this abundance when afternoon looms
like a bony forearm thrown across
the beginning of the moon, ill portent,
animal dead in the road—

no matter. This morning in my reading,
Darwin found the Andes, climbed higher
than his shipmates to the fossils of the sea things
in the cliffs, lifted his face to blue

and did not panic, as I believe he will
in later days, journey over and infirmities
besetting him, God too close to be forgotten
and the creatures in a museum

in London, packed in cotton and smelling of rot.
Let Darwin have his day
in the Andes, the first flush of freedom
from salvation upon him, the world revealing

its face in the thin air like green over the choppy sea.
Let me have my small pleasures: love
in the afternoon, the dog who cries to go out
and is let out, the words that arrive

like mysteries—like the gift of a bone-white
shell in rock four thousand feet above the sea,
silence leading into silence, the Englishman
who slips his god from the Ark,

sensing only that the wind is fresh
and up today, feeling only the weight
in his hands of the spiraled things
and the ache in his legs from climbing so far.

Field Trip

I went to jail with my fourth-grade class.
The trip was only meant to scare us
from small lives of crime—our teachers
didn't mean to show us what they did,
the beds like cordwood cut and stacked for cold,
the men alone in cages who looked at us
as though they couldn't get enough.
We scattered after high school, some of us
to waiting farms and some to towns
where we could finally feel alone.
But one night in the backseat of a dented
Chevy bellied to the curb on Mott,
I realized what the men in jail had wanted:
they didn't want to look through bars
at our small faces, but for us to look
at them. What's more, they left us carrying
their need: when we were brought out blinking
from the dark grey belly of the jail,
we had been taken by desire, marked
with it like ashes on the forehead, a smear
of promise we could barely understand.
Ruined, we were not to be the mother
leaning in to watch her child breathe,
but instead the blood that takes a left
turn at the heart and makes a circle
for the grateful, dazzled brain. I hoped
you saw my foot rise up
to slap the glass or heard him call out,
guessing at my name. I wanted you
to sit up later in your darkened room,
to see again that crappy Chevy rocking

on its metal hips, knowing
you can see, the way a woman late
at night might leave her shades
undrawn, and then pretend to be alone.

Babysitting

We thought it was gross, and funny, and said we'd never babysit in that house again, and anyway the twins were brats and there was no tv. Lila was the prettiest in our class, like in the Billy Joel songs we agreed were written just for her. She got a locket for her birthday from her boyfriend, who hung it on her neck on the bus ride home while we watched from sticky plastic seats. He kissed her after, gently. We called Mr. Ellison *perv,* and felt sorry for the twins, whose dad was such a dork. We didn't think of Lila in the darkened car, wearing the locket that marked her Lucky, waiting for Mr. Ellison to move his hand, hoping he thought it was resting on the seat, her bag with her math book in it, anything but the thing that he was teaching her. We told it at slumber parties, not having yet discovered what it is to have been picked, the dark space that opens up between the choosing and the way you choose to tell, the way your life can separate into two halves and never come back to you, the flush of confusion to be lucky, to be chosen, to be these things and also feel this way.

The Game

My brother the pitcher was skinny and anxious, dangerous without ever meaning harm. On Saturdays, we took our places on the lawn with my father. My job was to represent the batter, which frightened us both. My father remained unreadable under his Charlotte Indians hat. The ball was smooth, as hard as a stone. My brother wanted to control it. His desire narrowed the distance between *pitch* and *hit* until, inevitably, the target was struck. I walked it off without talking about it, following my father's instructions. I tasted the sting on my skin, then a low ache that entered my body and claimed a place in my life. Each failed pitch made my brother angrier, his good intentions leaving him like light out of a window. Each bright mark from contact made me love him, in bewilderment, more.

First Dead

In the end, it wasn't Buster or the cornering school bus that killed the Foster's dog, but the milkman, his rounded toy-truck just big enough to drop a bouncing retriever in its tracks, tongue still out for barking and the good taste of the morning chase. Danny found the dog by the spot where we waited for the bus, its coat dust over gold, one maroon trail snailing from its open mouth. We eyed our own small mutt, who would not smell the dead, who pressed close when we boarded the bus then lay by door, my mother said, until we got home. By then we were full of the small injustices of the day, the Foster's dog forgotten, bagged and driven to some dark building, replaced by a succession of labs who all died by bloat from stealing at the compost pile. Pearl survived our childhoods, grew deaf and blind and trembled when she walked, loved by then only by my mother, who put ribbons around each soft ear the day the vet came whistling with his black satchel down the long dirt road for the dog.

Route 7

The policeman pulled us over on old Route 7, just miles from home. He held his flashlight forward in two hands, the shock of yellow in our father's station wagon like the lines that sometimes fall through cloudy days and pitch the Little League game into a left-field finger of light. Then my sister sleeping in the back seat woke up screaming, and even after we didn't get arrested or have to call our parents, and got to keep our shoes on standing under the hot moon while the policeman pored over the seats and crickets called just off the road, she cried and wouldn't explain herself. Danny drove the rest of the way slowly with his backbone hunched, his week-old old license shoved back in his jeans. In the driveway, Rachel finally answered me—*I dreamt we were old. We were at Danny's funeral*—then went into the house through the fritzing electric front-porch light.

Turning Back

The grandmother, for example, has stilled her motions so close to zero that her arms no longer work to feed her. Young nurses spoon food into her mouth at meal times. In the yellow afternoons, she lies as still as a blanket stretched tight on an empty bed. Yet when the emergency comes—pneumonia or the stroke—she panics and comes back. Afterwards she is always these two things: furious, and hungry.

The Wolfman's Sister

Though cast as lady or grotesque,
as hectic membrane in the flesh,
she would not be neither-nor.

—Alice Fulton

I was the child wrapped in a red cloak,
knuckles on my shoulders
turning me to face the forest.
A slight push, only a tiny one
to set my feet on the path,

unwind the string, re-gather
the breadcrumbs, and get it right
this time; or this: to be the girl
he wanted, but the prayers held
not together in that light.

When I was twelve I tried to disappear,
to slip away without notice
into smooth, resistant bone.
Our mother fed me sweets
and tiny cakes, filling my mouth

and kissing it shut, sighing
in my ear, *so take dominion, take—*
So I became a still life
in a glass bowl and then a window

to be looked through, landscape
as far as the eye could see. I traveled
deep inside of it, but the woods
rose up and became a corridor lit
with footfalls each night and every

night, forevermore—my cloak slips
from my shoulders and it sighs a red
fall *brother can't you see that*
I am burning?—think of ashes
in the dispassion of the morning,

a cool grey coating over grass; and when
you kneel to sift it through your hand
like sand, it gives up nothing,
not a whisper or a chip of bone,
just particle and drift already gone.

Confession

I walked into a James Turrell piece. I stood in it,
I say it here: once I made my little sister sit
in dog shit, I pick my nose most days, I took off
my shoes and slid across the museum floor

in my socks, over the black tape line to the
blue blue blue of the double box glowing
like a nightbird diner. Once I got high
in the afternoon just to read the giant MOBIL

sign when the sun went down and the neon
came up in the sky. I wasn't alone, by the way,
not to excuse myself, but my companions
were all artists and should have known better.

Everybody knows that poets have no
boundaries. I did once steal a boyfriend's letters
to read the one that called him cold "except
your body, which you can't help."

There was a camera, and we took turns
posing gravely in the blue. I held
your hand so we could go together.
Once I killed a kitten because I thought

they always landed on their feet, but
I was three so I've forgiven myself for that one,
as well as the fact that I do always take
the front seat in the car. Do I think I'm better

than everyone else was a fair enough question
put to me by a man on a flight to Alaska
when I opened a book during the summation
of his plan for a Manhattan commuter helicopter.

The Turrell piece was in a museum in Napa.
I still have the picture. You and I
are silhouettes with our arms out, pasted up
on blue like something you might see

out the window of a plane if angels existed,
featureless happiness glowing at its edges.
I left you after I promised you I never would,
and I met James Turell and did not tell him

I'd been in his work. So here it is, although
I have to say we passed the guard on our way out,
flushed faces and laces flapping, and she smiled;
she knew human nature as well as anyone: we are made

to promise things to one another under the firm duress
of wanting, promises we drop like coins
in every puddle, expecting a return;
promises we never meant to keep.

Dancing

We were all night at a party
in a warehouse by the docks
where you danced Big Bird Walks
and Oscar Rises from His Can,
dipping me low while the floor
rose up and night reaching forward
spun us so all I could see
was the blur your body made
leaving one place for another
the way an animal smells footprints
in the snow, understanding
everything about the heel
and toes that left the mark—
the story of the rough pad,
the broken nail,
if it was hungry or old—
understanding everything
but where the animal
who left the mark, the beautiful
animal, went afterwards.

Graduate School

For a while, it's the funniest story you've ever heard, funnier than Nicole trying to climb off the plane over Texas jacked up on champagne and valium and the handsome steward as he laid her down but this one is told by your lover, the one who slept with his professors and so now is sleeping with you, who nights is smoking in your bed with a single-minded joy that could never be American, moody over vagaries in Hegel in a way that could never be American, and sexual in a way that, as far as you can tell, is entirely not American. The story? He was eighteen, his first trip to America, was working as a greeter at the gates of Disneyland. He went to the bathroom for a cigarette and in the next stall over, someone was grunting on their toilet, loudly urging on the effort like a dog with a bone, so he looked and saw, beneath the bright red short pants puddled on the floor, the two gigantic plastic feet in Mickey's yellow shoes. Later you will find out he does lines off the head of Foucault on the hardcover edition of *Discipline and Punish* and that the men who followed him from bars were acting on a solid hunch, and he will say that he can never live in America because of the death penalty—which is very different than a harmless Mickey taking a dump, and far more permanent —and then he will say the lines "I want to be with you but never in the same apartment," so you will pack your bags and go back to America where you will fall in with a banker from Connecticut who will hurt you in ways your European could never have imagined, having not grown up with that particular American dream of being given all you ever wanted by parents who regret you; but all of that is later, is arriving but not yet, for now you are in a bar in Europe and a man is telling the funniest story you have ever heard, and you are thinking how he will come back to your lonely flat and transform you all night long, how he will speak to you in languages you don't understand, until, dazzled, you for-get yourself what it means to come from a country where your grandparents came as children to escape starvation, that kills its criminals and pays good money for men to dress as Mickey Mouse. You won't understand his story until much later, when you hear that he has moved to New York on the dime of a university and you think of his America being Mickey taking a shit, and finally you ask yourself why he didn't just speak to you in English, and why it was so important to say Goethe right, and then you think of him, eighteen in America, shaking hands with Americans in brightly colored polo shirts and shorts and how sometimes it is not enough to want the right thing, not when you are hungry or alone, not when you are offered something you didn't even know you needed until the moment it is given, and after that you let your mind go blank and you take it.

Giving You Back the Musée d'Art

The show was the teeming darkness
of video: visions flashing like starlings
over the ceiling and walls, an overheated
room, a set of stairs, a chair, a woman

on a porch, blue sky through glass,
nothing lining up for its turn but jostling
the brain unhitched to let the world
come in hard without mercy.

I was sick from the teeming, staggered
to the lobby, and had to sit with my head down
for an hour until I could drive—
For once let's tell it right. You were driving.

You were driving and the blizzard came
as we drove south, white wind
and double fists of snow thinning the road
to something squeezed from a tube,

the world nothing on either side of us.
All the long ride home, Canada cracking
under the weight of the freeze, Vermont
a pinpoint swimming in black, and penitence

already beginning to drive us apart,
we practiced our stories, threaded our lies
so well that for all these years
when I described the video exhibit

I saw in Canada—the details of confusion
and the dark—I myself forgot that you
were there. Finally, here: your fingers
slipping past elastic, mouth on the back

of my neck, a chair, a woman on a porch,
blue sky through glass, Montreal poised
at the precipice of a storm.
Now that I don't feel this, I remember.

Wedding Poem

That night I dreamt I killed a dwarf.
At first, it seemed it was an accident,
but then my dream self murmured,

I did get away with the first two,
so maybe this time I should turn myself in...
I went to a party but didn't enjoy myself.

The space where the dwarf had been
loomed everywhere, making a shape in the world
of a small and absent body.

My guilt filled the shape exactly
and I began to hope
that they would come for me—

then I remembered your dark eyes secret
in sleep, your rough palms
pressed flat between dreams,

and a waking fierceness rising in me whispered,
let the dwarf stay dead.
Let its missing body sink into the fabric of earth

without a mark. Let good and evil shrink
to the size of a hand—
you have given them away.

I woke up beside you with the truth
inside me like a dream that follows your day.
I will never let you go.

Love Poem

My godmother wants to die, when her time comes,
by taxi. She plans to throw herself in the path
of a yellow cab on Park—she's confident

the driver will never think to use the brake.
She will be wearing her best suit, and my mother,
her oldest friend, will be there too, to smooth

her skirt sedately over her angled knees.
New York City will move around her,
traffic like water splitting around a rock

in a river, coming back to itself
unchanged. My godmother will lie on her corner
in her Chanel suit, resplendent

and splendid under the wheels of an unprotesting
cab on its way to pick up, or drop off,
just doing its business, which on one particularly

brilliant autumn afternoon,
sun working its way down the avenues
like light unfurling in tunnels, will include

lifting my godmother from the city she loves,
leaving just a vast and rippled wake, catastrophe
one thumbprint smeared and blurring.

Elegy I

The city existed in a fog to me then,
streets unfolding without warning, corners

turning into darkened alleys, subway stations
that brought you into daylight

blocks from where you thought you were.
You took me to a place on a sidewalk,

chalked a circle into the pitted cement.
Where we met! you finally said, exasperated.

The buildings were utterly unfamiliar, their windows blank faces.
Were we east or west of Union Square?

Already the child was beginning inside me.
This was another city still, secretive

and unavailable to mercy.
Its streets lay in impassable shadows, its doorways

unmarked on any maps we carried.
I didn't know this then. All I knew

was that I was lost and what I was beginning
to know: that you

were going to prove useless
for finding my way home.

II.

36   LEAVE IT BEHIND

Leave It Behind

I. Wolf

The wolf comes in July.
You open the door because you live

in a house in a meadow
and understand yourself to be

more than your body: bull thistle,
oxeye daisy, Klamath weed, fir;

marjoram on window shelves, baby's
breath behind the house, small

spots of dirt on the hands.
The wolf wears the costume

of a man, blue jeans and a shirt, but is
nettles and bloodwort,

beetles clacking, caws in the digger pines,
water pooling red as rust.

The wolf takes his costume off
and ruins your house,

meadow grass watching you run
with what looks like a dog at your back.

II. *Forest*

run through the thickets the river
to houses that buttress the hill

the blacktop to flag down a car I keep pushing
and dragging you pulling your arms

to make you run faster and almost
the blacktop the houses the yellow

of rescue I'm grateful and say so
you turn and fall backwards

just turning to check on the
breadcrumbs   spun into

the forest your loosening fingers
house yawning with sugar

eyes counting your knucklebones
moon on its side

your small brother watching
the dull steel of morning the grinding

and grinding he rattles the bars
and shouts at your braids standing out

in the wind for gods sake
stop running stop running lie down

III. Meadow

One winter the meadow behind
the little green house filled with beasts.
The snow in the high country
emptied the peaks, and coyotes came down
to look for their meals in the space
between frozen ground and snow.
They slept in tight bunches but ranged
winter mornings close to the house.

This was the winter of fires
in the stone fireplace, quick jig
to the outhouse, open tumblers
of jaegermeister at four pm.
We thought we might finally be animals
because we felt the outside world.

Then we began to wake before dawn
bristled by voices running like water
blue shadows heaped in the meadow
something like the cover of night
ringing the house, thick fur
standing up at the neck, noses
cocked for scent. We thought
it might be the animals, watching.

Night to us was coco in a mug, blood
running tender under the skin.
What did we know about anything?
Beyond the thin green walls
of the little house, a thump and toss
of brown, a flash of white escaping.

IV. Flight

She would like to lie down under the silken weight
of a man and not feel fear.

She would like to walk into the falling cape
of twilight alone.

She agrees it was like lightning: eighteen years old
and raised on myths;

reading after how she learned it, leaning in to love
the wings that took her.

No: it was like falling in the dark over a stone,
hidden until you trip.

Women, she knows, can sometimes be hurt
and learn to live easily again.

She will never live again without a dog to watch her
or, uneasily, a man.

V. City

I knew before I knew because I smelled him:
wet wool under the stairs
behind me, sticky locks, flat mailslots, nothing

for me there and he with his cheek
on the wall like a child,
fists tucked under his tipped-down chin.

I used to think (when I thought of what
it might have been like for you)
of jumping from the high rock over the river:

long enough in the air to regret the leap,
but then the landing
in the cool green pool, the quick swim to the edge,

the limbic system already on to other things.
But gripping my blunt and useless
keys in the company of my own adrenalin-scented

dark-eyed man, I realized it wasn't like the river
at all, and then I knew
what went on and on for you, the moves

from getting out unharmed to getting out at all
to simply maybe living;
and so I ran and I was saved, and only later did I think

about your message, which is something
I have been waiting for—
don't the dead ones always signal to those they left behind?

I was looking for peace like the flat of a sheet I could snap
over my head, or a light in the kitchen
that would not shift, something settling like hayseed

to let me know that you were fine, but instead
I got this one word: *run!* the way it must have felt
to have the angel bring the news:

filled to the rim with a blazing sight so absolute
and so unwelcome
that it doesn't seem to have a proper name.

VI. Field

Then one day, it was amazing, she escaped. Yes, sometimes it is like that. She got up from the broken-down ferns and shook her lovely shoulders back and ran, yes, she ran, faster than the dark wolf, faster than the stories they would tell about her later, her red hair burning behind her—that's how fast she ran, you see, so fast her hair caught fire, and her feet turned into wings, and her beautiful fingers flew up and away and she ran beyond the neighbor's house (which had been her goal, get to the house and he won't—) but no need, no, never anymore for the neighbor, or the men in windbreakers who dug up her garden, or the harnessed dogs that knew to go to the river; no, there never was a need for any of them, and they just stayed on in the city and never came— no, never came at all—and she ran until she was gone, not tired, just gone, and you may not know this, but I will tell you: the papers got it wrong—she did get away and she stayed there.

44 LEAVE IT BEHIND

III.

46   LEAVE IT BEHIND

I Love the Animals

So why do they keep charging me in my sleep?
Giant flies with human faces crowd

the air in the kitchen—I battle hard with a rolled-up
Times, but the flies fight back,

bumbling me toward strips uncurling
sticky from the ceiling, a rising

buzz and shoving, then the mercy
of awake in bed. Last night's dream closed

with tiny fuel-efficient cars, us racing
to get in one ahead of the mice,

who had swelled to pony-size and angry,
cramming themselves into every available space.

Of course you were there too, and when I dreamt
about our dog dying in the road outside

the house or hit in stopped-motion by the
passing truck, crying to be helped from pain

and I woke up in agony, you were there
too, stitched into the lexicon of outsized

truth that dreams deliver—your body opened
at its side with its crazy seams showing,

possible here to fear the one you love
—and both as real as dreams in which

the cage of fancy holds the real disease,
the latch for leaving smooth and hot, so real

that if your hand closed on it dreaming you'd step
through and, waking, find yourself in a new place,

the rules dismissed, the path home sewn with brambles,
and something buzzing, faintly, gone.

Lesson for Snake Charming

*Thus follows the question: is snake charming an art,
and if so, how is it acquired?*

—Ditmars' *Reptiles of the World*

The Naja is wrenched awake again, time and repetition
doing nothing to knit her threadbare nerves.
The glass caps balanced on her lidless eyes

fail to keep the world from entering her slightest dreams.
It's not the music—with her tongue to the breeze
she can hear the nervous heartbeat of a hesitating mouse,

so what could music mean to her? It's the body in motion
that pulls at her like a thousand strings hooked
in the keels of her scales, marshalling her every move.

Tortoise-colored, short-toothed serpent, Naja naja
of tales, as furious as if the first time thus disturbed—
this footpacked dirt, these frightened, lascivious faces,

smell of grease from last night's meal. The jerky movements
catch the hemstich of her sight, making her sick
from a sensation of reeling, an animal transfixed by the bit.

Her ribs spread out like shells releasing
the muscle within, her flattening hood a death's head
embroidered on a lady's square. The crowd convulses

as she opens to the trace his body makes in the air.
Her jaw aches for the doubled unfolding
of bones, the mute give of skin under her teeth.

The man throws a rooster and she strikes,
her point of fury safe behind the fluttered dying
in the puffs of dust. Then he is still

and she can't find him, the confidante
to Cleopatra drained to torpor, a fine hand
closed on this exactitude of wanting

and dust: butcher birds like dark priests
praying at the plate and the man who bends to spit
in the dirt, the marvelous charmer of snakes.

Fox Paws

Because I'm a total color-whore, I noticed the palate first in this
    piece—
grading thirty-seven art school essays in my living room,
I've been drinking since the middle of the pile; do they all
come high to my class? I know the three painters

who snack through the seminar, the ones I thought
were getting all my jokes, are actually thinking things like,
what if you were reading a book, and you opened it,
and the pages were blank, but you kept on reading anyway

cracking themselves up while I preen myself
at the far end of the table like the Sally Field of higher education.
Anna K. reminds me of my Mother god I hate that bitch.
Monday nights are Coco, reading from her freewrites—

a tiny blush and then the spanking scene with her girlfriend
on the roof of the dorm, or the three-way
on the folding couch while the band plays on in the kitchen.
Arden wears a hand-made pieced fur toga

and has a project going to knit every hour
she's awake for a year. She drags the yarn-mass
behind her like a filthy pet, lets us know the day
she can no longer fit on public transportation.

It's about a blackbird, I plead with them,
and argue that Edward Albee knew
his characters had issues with alcohol and self-esteem;
but they are out ahead of me, not afraid

to pierce themselves or change their gender: they know
Martha needed therapy, they know lovers
always come back. *It was clear from her face,*

one student reads in class, *that he had committed a major fox
    paws.*

The other students might be high, or just polite,
or maybe they recognize that art is malleable and is up
for grabs and a fox paw is just as good as fake French anyway,
but no one seems to mind; and so the fox paws

travel the path opened by the young man's voice,
trotting lightly toward the smell of sunlight,
to where the warm green song of a thrush gathers
in a puddle of velvet over a star-filled tree.

An Old Story

Jesus called up Lazarus
and it was amazing!
Crowds of people stood around

to watch him reappear.
Jesus said, "Lazarus," which meant
your body, and so the body

came forth: named-body, name-
of-body, body still blurry with dirt.
Lazarus woke in the body,

but something had changed.
His youngest child no longer knew him,
his dog growled at him in the door,

suddenly he hated fish. At night
when he entered the warm body
of his wife, who had fasted and wept

without stopping for three days
and nights, Lazarus felt something
slipping, as though his body

were rolling over the edges of the earth,
as though the earth itself
was not at all as it displayed itself

but instead was something rounded
and unknowable.
Lazarus began to drink at night,

staying out late until his name
slid away. His neighbors carried him home,
bleary and weeping, his robes dragging

in the dust. His skinny dog
crouched in the doorway, moving easily
when Lazarus swung a clumsy foot—

dumb beast, it didn't even run
but sat just out of reach
with its tongue out, laughing.

Early Freeze, Fairbanks

When Molly dragged home the fawn, perfect
as a teacup, its small feet
as round as spoons but softer,
she ate it to its bamboo bones
then licked the faint stains as they sank
away in unexpected early snow.
That night the rivers broke and froze,
crying their names through frazil closing:
Ester, Chena, Tok, Nenanna
under the whirring of a thousand wings
moving over the closing lattice, seeking
the warmth of solace near the house,
finding only Molly, crying to come in.

Elegy II

I thought of you the other night,
thinned the way you were the last time

by the unexpected demands of blood.
I too am thin, as empty as a handbag after thieves

have taken everything worth weight.
I try to write but I don't believe

in language like I used to—I'm reduced
to pointing, saying, *here, here, here,*

running my palms over the curves of the city
to claim them, that inheritance

that once was effortless
in the low light before we met

and taught each other
about the limits of speech,

the insistence of the body,
the fisted muscle of the heart.

The Doctor Only Heard One Heart

in their mother's womb
holding each other
neither she nor her sister remember
not yet born

the dumb animal of longing
two heartbeats synced to a pitch
without tides or waves
there would have been liquid darkness

there would have been liquid darkness
without tides or waves
two heartbeats synched to a pitch
the dumb animal of longing

not yet born
neither she nor her sister remember
holding each other
in their mother's womb

it's just a story told in the family.

At Seven They Say

that they can fool people
with their faces
but the mirror, faithless,
gives them otherwise:
green eyes to brown,
pale skin and hers
like a flush
from their Irish mother,
her small frame and hers
from their father.
They can't get
to what they know
to be the truth.
Then they are ten years old.
The world outside
them keeps insisting
like a palm insisting
its existence in a fist.

At Eleven They Fight

Why can't we—
  —Why can't we what?

(She can't say it)

  —Just say it!

(but she doesn't know what)

One draws a line down the center of the bedroom
while the other one watches.

At Twelve They Tear Apart

She has been locked out of the bathroom now
for three days and three nights—
the bathroom where they meet before bed
where they used to sit together on the toilet

back to back for the delight of naughtiness
    yes but more
for fitting on something really made for one.
Now she pounds her fists

on the faithless door:
    —*open the stupid door!*
(She is still afraid to swear because of God.)
Her sister opens the door and passes by her

as though she follows someone patiently
but cannot see the world, moving
to her side of the bedroom and sitting on the bed,
looking toward the window.

She finds the proof in the basement,
crumpled and shoved into a basket of dirty clothes
    so she has gone ahead again
but says nothing, and a few days later

her sister lets her back into the bathroom.
Then she bleeds
too and they are together again
but she does not forget

    forget how could she forget
the door closed to her, her sister's face
closed like an inlaid box,
the ease with which she took

her leave—
it is as she suspected it would be.

Her Nightmare

In it, her sister has died.

It has already happened, but they are allowed
to see each other one last time.

Her sister's hair falls in her face
as it did when they were children

and the barrette would slip
in her baby fine hair. She asks her sister:

    —Are you happy? Are you sad?
Her sister shakes her head

full of something else
that is not knowing

what wanting to be happy is,
or sad,

only the taste of waiting
to go back. Seeing finally

what she has always feared,
she quickly starts the story:

The Story

Imagine this, now
this: a pitch

in the liquid, a sudden twist
of longing—

> *she can't quite remember*
> *but she knows*

> *who came first,*
> *whose lungs folded*
> *in shock*

she waits in a house,
waits days

while her sister works
for air in a dim-lit tent—

> *but this is the part of the story*
> *she can't remember:*
> *did her sister want to come back*

> *or did the hunching tank insist on*
> *pouring air into her resolution, pinching*
> *salt for luck on her head?*

waits without looking,
breaks no rules,

believes she will return,
and then, and then—

> *but her sister in the dream wants*
> *nothing. Silence*
> *covers patience in her face.*

Spring, El Portal

I told you the story in the kitchen,
shouting over the shouting river.
You examined your hands,

the thin lines in your wrists
like the snaking of blue on a map,
then gave your apple a name and went hungry.

Outside, the Merced river churned,
a sullen Chinese river harnessed barely for rice.
Every day it rose further, crowded

with stones from the high country,
swallowing unsated the neighbors' dog,
two or three trailer homes,

the hotel bar built too close to its banks.
The story: Roger Williams died,
was buried, became an apple tree.

The people in Rhode Island
ate him every fall, inside the reddened skin
and sweet white crisp of the crop,

and when they dug him up to move his grave,
they found only roots
like limbs in the shape of a man.

That night the river entered our yard,
its long arms calling us awake.
We reached across that silent bed as water

jostled the doors then imitated lonely,
begging to come in. *After*
would be different—the house like a boat

barely moored, everything
cancelled for days
while the river called in its debts,

one of us gone by summer—
but that night we lay together
and let the river in. It didn't hurt

as we thought it might,
so we filled and filled our greedy mouths
as the water rose, dark, in the house.

Rain Is Black and White, Like a Photograph

It has a long memory, but cannot tell
its own stories: green river, gritty
run-off, black water in a lake.
Now, like the dead, it is all one thing.
Like the dead, it crowds
the windows, even as we think
that we are looking out.
All this changes, we admit, gesturing
at the window where even now
the rain is beating harder
than it was this morning.
But we whisper to ourselves. I remain
the same. Rain pounds
on the skylight, washing helplessly
from the point of the roof to the ground
like a singular thing.

Milestone

Yesterday is not a milestone that has been passed,
but a daystone on the beaten track of the years
and irremediably part of us, within us,
heavy and dangerous.

—Samuel Beckett

We arrived at this place in the woods: green,
quiet, no peaked roof in our line of sight.
Our hearts were silver in our chests, our bodies
as good as though we had four legs and slept

in the thickets of soft branches at night.
The blood in our veins was the whirring
warning of hurried wings over slowing rivers,
but we didn't know to head south

so what we conjured answered, gathered
like clouds in front of thunder and arrived.
Then the dark house rose like mud on a riverbank,
windows yellow ovals in the night.

We waited at the knob and were let in,
a single mercy for the cold and frightened.
You were there so long, a favorite
long after I had sold my knucklebones for bread.

Given one small window, you could see the forest
but it was stripped and bare, receding
in a shrinking aperture towards language—poor
mimic. You gripped memory like a stone

in your fist, clenched it to make
what might have happened speak to you.
But remember? Memory is water
when held in a fist—runs out, heads for earth.

The Hinge

The bat on the table has the face of a baby,
button nose and round brown eyes
when he thumbs them open. It's June twenty-two
in the Downs, the longest day of the year.

The knees are indeed backwards, made
to bend behind the bat, walking sticks
for hanging upside-down. Darwin says
articulus but, once again, it's what we don't know

that will find us; and the word, which also means
"a hinge," takes fire as it leaves his mouth
on this night, the pivot in the ancient solar year.
The body, he muses, looks familiar

but as in a tale to frighten children:
the fingers as long as the nightmare hair
on the fairy-tale baby, the tiny, clutching
feet not palm like bear or toe like fox,

the leathered reach of unfeathered wings
as in a dream of hovering, poised forever
between flight and ground. *Articulus,*
the scientist murmurs, England's

own magician of shells and bones.
The study darkens for a moment as if night
has been pulled in with a drawstring,
light gone red at the window, the creak

in the house the conjured hinge of the year.
Upstairs, Emma is weeping.
She creases again the letter she has written
that tells her husband there are things

we cannot see and simply must believe;
describes her incurable grief—*if I thought*
we did not belong to each other forever—her faith
a pebble carried always in her mouth.

Darwin notes his findings in the number
seven notebook. Emma folds
the coverlet back for night.
The doubled-jointed envoy on the table

stirs and whiskers out the window,
the light of a thousand bonfires pricked
in its eyes. Fingertips slip the sky
on the dotted line, breaking the seal between

the dark door waiting and the neighbor's
terrified pets—messenger not skin or wing
but something in between, like between
the window and the frame or the humans

and the silent world that waits,
the yellow space that brightens briefly
for the truly watchful just before
the door is gently, firmly closed.

Self-portrait as a House

If I were a house, I'd be a little
green house, with peeling paint
and an Ali Baba stairway
to my swinging green screen door.

If I were this house, I'd have
one floor, so no one would be lost
testing the stairs after sundown
to see where they reached.

Once safe across my lintel,
the ones I love make fires
with magically appearing wood,
eat food in the kitchen from cupboards

that refill themselves each night.
Outside are seasons, and wolves in rings,
and the pitiless moon
on a cloudless night who watches;

but inside the little green house,
it will always be not night and not yet
morning pushing at the glass,
music playing in the living room,

and people eating in a yellow light
like lamplight who love each other
fiercely and yet cannot remember
how they met or if they are related

or how they came to live
in the little green house with the strange
innumerable bedrooms, animals
walking in and out at dusk, and windows

of an odd clear glass that lets in light
but only shows an endless meadow
all around the house: not sunlight,
and not real grass, but

two things that, when looked at from
a distance, show themselves to be
what you need, or what you thought
you did when all of this began.

A Dream of Horses

For Paul

In the dream it started to snow: slow
unfettered clouds drifting through the sky
without direction, an unguided flight
until the flakes began to settle
an arched neck, dark flank, cocked
fetlock filled in slowly line by line,
gently coaxed into arriving
as a field of horses resting
under robes of snow; and what had been
invisible shone forward into sight—
what was hidden, what was blurred with night
made clear, brought into shape by light.

The Other Story

she is not telling.
Or, rather, she knows not
what to tell. She has always
had nightmares, seen shapes

in the bedroom, raged
against anything that leaves
or is taken; always she is mourning
or stealing, aware

that she is the darker one.
But that's a stupid story, like twins
brought to sickbeds for cure
or left in forests for beasts

or someone who travels
to drag back an unwilling—
she can't say because she won't
think about that long journey,

not allowed to look back
although her shoulder muscles
strain to twist. She has to just
believe her sister follows her, wants

to come up from that soft place, wants
to feed her in her stupid grief
for things that have not yet
even come. She could fill

a room with that grief and still
have plenty left.
In this, she is alone.

The Mirror

In the bathroom before bed
they make moles with a magic marker,

one on each side of her mouth,
like hers,

and put the extra pair of glasses
on her.

Finally
standing quiet in the mirror

are the twins,
their secret visible,

just touching in the glass.
This is what

they have been waiting for:
not a reflection

but her,
a perfect likeness.

They want this.
This
                    is what I want.

Acknowledgments

"Fox Paws," "Self-portrait as a House," *FutureCycle Poetry*, 2011

"An Old Story," *Indiana Review*, Fall 2008

"The House in the Meadow," *Big Ugly Review*, Fall 2008

"Babysitting," "The Game," "Route 7," "Turning Back," *Chelsea*, 80,
    June 2006

"My Best Dream," *Sow's Ear Poetry Review*, Spring 2006

"Darwin in the Andes," *The Alaska Quarterly Review*, Fall 2005

"Spring, El Portal," *Gulf Coast*, Spring 2005

"Milestone," *The Crab Orchard Review*, Winter 2005

"Rain is Black and White, Like a Photograph," *The Antioch Review*,
    Fall 2004

"Love Poem," *Agni Online*, May 2004

"Driving Without Headlights," *The Brooklyn Review*, No. 16, 1999

Leave It Behind came in second place in the judging for the 2011
FutureCycle Poetry Book Prize, FutureCycle Press.

☙

The author would like to thank the Ragdale Foundation and the
MacDowell Colony for the gift of time to write. Thanks also to her
trusted readers—Randall Potts, Ramsay Breslin, Alison DeLauer,
and Alison Powell—and her family for their unending support.

*Cover artwork, "Andover," by Allison Gildersleeve; author
"painting" from a photo by Lawrence LaBianca; cover design
and typography by Diane Kistner; Cambria text with Century
Gothic titling*

The FutureCycle Poetry Book Prize

FutureCycle Press conducts an annual full-length poetry book competition open to any poet writing in the English language. The winning manuscript is published in both print and digital formats, with the poet receiving a $1,000 prize plus 25 copies of the published book. (Finalists may also be offered publishing contracts; those published are listed below.) Submissions of book manuscripts for the contest are accepted from January 1 to April 15 of each year for that year's competition. Non-contest book and chapbook submissions are considered year-round, but the book competition takes precedence. We also publish individual poems in *FutureCycle Poetry,* our online magazine. These poems, which remain online indefinitely, are collected into an annual print edition each November. All submissions must be received via our online submission form to be considered. To avoid unnecessary delays or unread returns, poets should review our guidelines at www.futurecycle.org.

———

FutureCycle Poetry Book Prize Winners
Mosslight by Kimberley Pittman-Schulz (2011)
Stealing Hymnals from the Choir by Timothy Martin (2010)
No Loneliness by Temple Cone (2009)

———

FutureCycle Poetry Book Prize Finalists
Leave It Behind by Emily Raabe (2011)
Castaway by Katherine Riegel (2010)
Simple Weight by Tania Runyan (2010)
Luminous Dream by Wally Swist (2010)
Beyond the Bones by Neil Carpathios (2009)

Full-length Books
The Porous Desert by David Chorlton
Violet Transparent by Anne Coray

Chapbooks
Colma by John Laue
The Secret Life of Hardware by Cheryl Lachowski
Scything by Joanne Lowery
A Love Letter to Say There Is No Love by Maria Russell-Williams

---

FutureCycle Poetry Anthologies
Please refer to our catalog for all *FutureCycle Poetry* editions
and other special anthology projects:
www.futurecycle.org

www.ingramcontent.com/pod-product-compliance
Lightning Source LLC
LaVergne TN
LVHW021118080426
835509LV00021B/3432